The United States Emerges

1783–1800

SADDLEBACK
EDUCATIONAL PUBLISHING

Saddleback's *Graphic American History*

SADDLEBACK
EDUCATIONAL PUBLISHING
www.sdlback.com

Copyright © 2009, 2010 by Saddleback Educational Publishing

All rights reserved. No part of this book may be reproduced in any form or by any means, electronic or mechanical, including photocopying, recording, scanning, or by any information storage and retrieval system, without the written permission of the publisher. SADDLEBACK EDUCATIONAL PUBLISHING and any associated logos are trademarks and/or registered trademarks of Saddleback Educational Publishing.

ISBN: 978-1-59905-358-5
eBook: 978-1-60291-686-9

Printed in Malaysia
25 24 23 22 21   9 10 11 12 13

In 1781, the Articles of Confederation were approved by the colonies, making the Continental Congress the official governing body of the country. Also in 1781, the Battle of Yorktown decided the outcome of the Revolution. American colonies had defeated the British.

General George Washington talked with Robert Morris, in charge of finance.

Sir, I must have money for the Army!

General, we are the governing body of the nation.

We have the power to make war—but no power to vote taxes to pay for it!

We must ask the states for money, and they don't pay us!

Very well! I will write the state governors.

Washington had refused to accept pay for himself, but he knew his men could not afford to do this.

There is no prospect of obtaining pay until part of the money required of the states can be brought into the public treasury.

You cannot conceive the uneasiness which arises from the total want of so essential an Article as Money.

He talked with James McHenry, an ex-officer, now a member of the Maryland legislature.

Each state is anxious to see the end of our warfare accomplished, but shrinks when it is called upon for means.

The revolutionary slogan, *No taxation without representation,* was taken to mean "No taxation—period!"

Young Alexander Hamilton, an aide to Washington for most of the war, led an important attack at Yorktown. Soon after, he left the Army and returned to his wife and family in Albany, New York.

Darling, at last you are here! I am so happy!

I am through with public life! From now on I want nothing but to be with my family.

But Robert Morris felt differently.

You know our need for money. I want you to be collector of our taxes for New York State.

No! I want to practice law.

The need is desperate! You know the situation in the Army. You have influence in New York.

Very well, sir. I'll try.

Hamilton sailed down the river to Poughkeepsie, where the legislature was meeting.

He met the governor and the committee on taxation. He proposed a tax plan that would help both the state and the nation.

Mr. Hamilton, it's a good plan, but we can't present it to the legislature.

They won't vote for it.

As a citizen, I am mortified that this state pays nothing in support of the war!

Congress had asked New York for $365,000. Hamilton collected $6,250. And other states did worse!

The legislature would not pass Hamilton's tax plan, but they passed another measure.

I move that Alexander Hamilton be sent as a representative to Congress.

All in favor say *aye*.

Hamilton went home to Albany and explained to his wife.

I wanted to stay out of public life. But our nation will collapse unless something is done to give us a strong federal government.

As Hamilton knew, there was great unrest in the Army. It had been a long time since men or officers had been paid.

Now the fighting's over, they don't care what happens to us.

If we give up our weapons, disband and go home, they'll never pay us.

But what can we do?

We fought the war—why should we suffer?

Maybe we could seize land and set up our estate.

Maybe we could make General Washington our king!

Washington received a letter from a respected officer, Colonel Nicola, suggesting they make Washington a king. He was terribly shocked.

No man possesses a more sincere wish to see justice done than I. But you could not have found a person to whom your schemes are more disagreeable.

But plans for mutiny continued to circulate. An unsigned folder called for a secret meeting of all officers. Washington issued an order forbidding secret meetings and set a time for another open meeting at which he would speak.

The officers assembled, and Washington made a long and moving address, appealing to their loyalty. They were not convinced. Then he pulled out a letter. He could not read the writing, and he stopped and put on his glasses.

Gentlemen, you must pardon me. I have grown gray in your services and now find myself growing blind.

They had never seen him wear glasses before. The simple words moved many to tears. They voted overwhelmingly their confidence in Congress and their patriotism.

Washington insisted to Congress that each man sent home should at least have three months' pay in his pocket. But, as always, he received the same answer.

General, there simply is no money! The best I can do is to give each man a note calling on his home state to give him three months' pay.

Troops in camp near Philadelphia petitioned Congress, refusing to go home without payment. Congress ignored their petition. Three days later 300 men entered Philadelphia and surrounded the building where Congress was meeting.

We'll give you 20 minutes to meet our demands. Otherwise, we're coming in after you.

In an ugly mood, the mutineers seized the arsenals.

Hamilton hurried to Governor Dickinson.

Supporters of Congress urged that they move out of the reach of the rioters. When the rioters heard that loyal troops were on the way from New York, they broke up. Congress later agreed to pardon them and shipped funds for their pay.

For several years, both Congress and states had been printing paper money with no gold and silver to back it up. The value of these paper dollars fell to nothing. There was terrible inflation. Under the Articles of Confederation, the nation was a group of individual states, each trying to do its own thing, with no one empowered to take charge.

A farmer and his wife owed a tax bill.

How much money have we got?

Hard money or paper money?

Dollars! I know we haven't enough hard money to count.

There's $300 here—your militia pay.

Wish it was $300 of hard money.

I've never gotten it through my head why paper dollars aren't as good as hard money since the Congress puts them out.

Because there's no hard money to back them up. This paper is American dollars, not British shillings and pounds. And there's no American shillings or pounds to back up the dollars.

But when the farmer went to pay his taxes, he was in for a shock.

This money's only worth two cents on the dollar. This $300 is worth $6 but your bill's $12.

But I did $300 worth of work.

Instead of using money, people traded something they had for something they needed—a system known as *barter*.

Our farmer went to see a hunter friend.

Can you lend me some furs to pay my taxes with and let me work it out?

Sure! You can work a day or two on the new barn I'm building.

In Rhode Island, the state assembly passed a law that paper money must be accepted at its face value. This caused other problems.

A pound of coffee beans, please.

That'll be one dollar hard money.

I have only paper money, and the law says you must accept it.

But the shipper makes me pay hard money for it! I'll be forced out of business.

Shopkeepers closed their doors rather than sell for the worthless paper. Angry shoppers rioted and broke in.

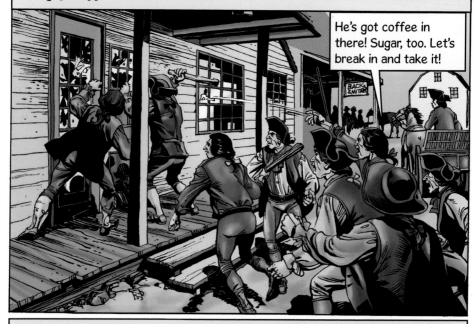

He's got coffee in there! Sugar, too. Let's break in and take it!

Some states, to raise money, put a tax on goods brought in from another state.

The miller a few miles down the road will trade me flour for this firewood.

But he lived in Connecticut, and the miller lived in New York State. One day he found a tax collector at the state line.

New York has an import tax now. You can't bring in that firewood without paying a tax.

But I live right down the road!

In western Massachusetts, things were very bad. State taxes were high. People had to go into debt to pay them. Then their land and homes were sold to pay their debts.

If you take my land and my house and my cows, how'll I support my children?

It's not right! What did we fight for?

If a man could not pay his debts, he was tried and imprisoned if guilty.

There's 92 of us here, all for owing money.

In the fall of 1786, mobs of farmers prevented the courts from sitting in the western counties.

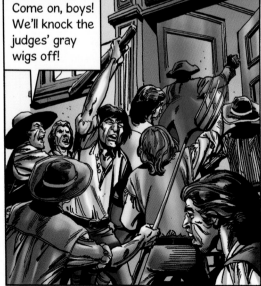

Come on, boys! We'll knock the judges' gray wigs off!

The angry men held county conventions, drew up petitions to the legislature, and set up committees of correspondence to keep in touch with each other. They wanted to stop judgments for debt and taxes until a new legislature could be elected.

But conservative Governor Bowdoin would not listen.

I'm issuing a proclamation against unlawful gatherings—and calling out the militia to break them up!

The men needed a leader. A committee called on Captain Daniel Shays, a Revolutionary War veteran.

Daniel, we need you for a leader!

We want to march on Springfield.

We have to stop the Supreme Judicial Court from meeting to indict our leaders.

I don't like it. It's treason.

It's no more treason than what the patriots at Lexington did!

In January, Shays led 1,100 men to the Springfield armory, where they hoped to get arms. The county militia, under General Shepherd, defended the armory.

Forward, on the double!

Fire the cannon.

Twice, the militia fired over the heads of Shays' men. They continued to advance. A third shot went into their ranks. Three men were killed. The others broke and ran.

A fresh militia army arrived and chased the rebels through the snow. Many were captured. Shays escaped to Vermont. Fourteen leaders were sentenced to death but later were pardoned. The new legislature granted some of their demands.

In Europe, there was great interest at news of an armed revolt in Massachusetts. The European powers believed that the United States would not survive long as a nation.

The English Tories were delighted to read of it.

Ah-ha! The Americans will never make a success of it. They'll beg to come back to us.

John Adams of Massachusetts was the minister to England. He talked it over with his wife, Abigail.

The English believe we have a fatal illness—but it is only growing pains!

King George had received Adams at court politely.

We were the last to consent to the separation... but we will be the first to meet the friendship of the United States as an independent power.

But later, the king turned his back on Adams and ignored him, and the courtiers followed suit.

It was Adams' job to work out treaties for trading with the British. But the foreign minister replied to him sarcastically.

They need not pour large armies into the United States. They can distress us more by cutting off all our trade.

Can your government enforce a treaty—or must we sign 13 treaties with 13 separate colonies?

British ports were closed to American ships and American trade, including the West Indies, where we had had an important market. On the other hand, English ships came to American ports and sold their goods far below the prices of American-made goods. And Congress had no power over the trade regulations of the individual states.

Several terms of the peace treaty caused trouble between England and the United States. Thousands of American Tories had left with the British troops at the end of the war. Their large land-holdings had been seized by the states, broken up, and sold to Americans. The British insisted that the Tories be paid for the land.

But sir, we agreed to recommend this to the states, which we have done. We did not claim to be able to force them to do it.

And what of the slaves and the American ships that were taken away and sold by your troops?

Well, yes, we admit that was illegally done.

The most serious problem involved the Canadian border posts on territory ceded to the United States. These forts controlled the valuable fur trade and the Native American threat in the Northwest Territory. Canada did not want the British troops to give them up.

They use as an excuse the fact that we are breaking the treaty in the matter of Tory debts. But I am convinced they never intend to give up the forts!

And while they hold the forts, our western settlers are in danger from the Indians!

Few people knew more about the western lands or the Native Americans than Daniel Boone, the wilderness scout.

What's Kentucky like, Daniel?

Why, there's mighty forests, and rich meadows.

There's plenty of game, so a man can take skins by the thousand. There's springs and streams and rivers.

There's more kinds of birds than I ever thought to see. I guess heaven's a Kentucky kind of a place.

Daniel had hunted in Kentucky. He had been captured by Native Americans there and had escaped. He had made up his mind to settle there. One day he was approached by Richard Henderson, an old friend.

Daniel, I understand you know of an Indian trail over the mountains into Kentucky.

That's right, Colonel, the Warriors' Trace.

I want you to take 30 men and cut out a road for me over the trace—one that wagons can follow.

I don't know about wagons, but I can cut out a good trail.

To Daniel Boone, Kentucky meant freedom, fine hunting, and a few settler-friends to help face the wilderness dangers. Henderson thought of money, power, and a great land-empire that he would control.

We'll call it Transylvania. I'll sell land to settlers, rent some of it. I'll give you 2,000 acres for your services, Daniel.

But doesn't Virginia claim ownership of the Kentucky lands?

The Indians owned it first. I'll buy title to it from the Indians.

Henderson and his partners persuaded the Cherokee tribes to come to a meeting at Sycamore Shoals. Over a thousand warriors and their families gathered there. They feasted on meals provided by the Colonel. They looked at the wagonloads of goods with which he would pay for the land—$50,000 worth.

My friends, it is all for you, my honored guests. There'll be plenty of sterling and goods—after the treaty is signed.

The council meeting began at sun-up. Colonel Henderson made a fine speech offering to buy the Native American hunting grounds. Everything seemed settled, but then an angry Dragging Canoe rose to his feet.

The young warrior spoke. He begged the tribal leaders not to sign away their hunting grounds.

My brothers, if you put your names to this paper, where shall we hunt? How shall we feed our children? Are we to be bought with money and goods?

His words echoed. He stalked away. The tribesmen leaped to their feet and followed him, chanting and yelling.

Daniel, can we do anything?

Spread out a big feast. Set out the goods and show them off.

But will they sign? I must have everything legal.

What else can they do? They can take your deal and get a little for the land, or wait a few years and have it taken away. They're smart enough to see that.

The Cherokees did sign. And the Colonel and his partners felt they were the legal owners of Kentucky.

But other men were interested in Kentucky, Ben Logan among them.

I'm going to Kentucky, Daniel. But I don't go along with the Colonel.

That's for you to decide. Ben, we're friends anyhow!

Why don't you come along with me and stake out a claim under Virginia law.

No, I'll stick with the Colonel. His money and backing will give things a push.

Daniel and his men went to work, blazing and cutting, cleaning underbrush, creating what would become the Wilderness Road. At last they came to Cumberland Gap.

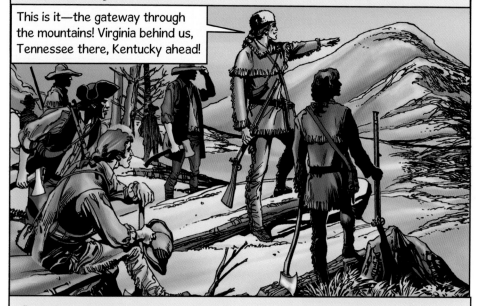

This is it—the gateway through the mountains! Virginia behind us, Tennessee there, Kentucky ahead!

Soon many settlers came over Daniel's road—those who bought land from Henderson's Transylvania Company and others like Ben Logan.

Virginia law says this 400 acres will be mine in a year, because of this cabin I'm building...

... and this crop I'm raising.

I reckon it's worth all the work you've done.

Many settlers like Ben Logan homesteaded their land and brought their families out, taking a chance that Virginia's law would prevail over Henderson's purchase. They built forts for protection when Native American attacks threatened.

In the fort at Logan Station, they were awakened one night by gunshots and a pounding on the stockade gate.

Who is it?

Hey, you Kentuckians! Open up!

It's Billy the scout!

Boys, Virginia has claimed title to the country. They've set it up as a new county, Kentucky County!

You hear! We've won! Just what we wanted!

What about the Colonel?

The legislature voted him down. He is trying to make them pay him some money for his trouble.

Colonel Henderson was later given 200,000 acres of land as compensation. But Daniel Boone never received his 2,000 acres.

To the western settlers, Congress seemed far away and little concerned with their problems. But in the 1780s, by passing the Northwest Ordinances, Congress took action that would affect the lives of all settlers west of the mountains, and the whole later development of the continental United States.

Robert Morris, finance minister, explained the problem.

The Congress is desperate for money. If the states claiming western lands would give up their rights, we could sell the land to benefit the entire nation.

Virginia cedes her claims to all land beyond the Ohio River!

Hear, hear!

Thomas Jefferson persuaded Virginia to go along.

Most states agreed to give up their claims. Then Jefferson headed a committee to draft a public land policy.

It is basically important that new states be formed and admitted to the Union on an equal basis with the original states.

The Ordinance that finally was passed embodied this principle. It also specified how townships should be laid out, how governments should be set up, and how a territory could become a state.

★ ★ ★

It provided for a bill of rights and for public education. It prohibited slavery in the Northwest Territory. And it provided a pattern for the great tracts of land the country would acquire.

John Jay, a young New Yorker, was sent to Spain when Spain became an ally. Arriving in Cadiz, he was welcomed by Count O'Reilly.

My dear Mr. Jay, you and your wife will be welcome at my home.

Thank you, but we must travel on to Madrid as soon as possible.

But for the journey you must hire a coach and six mules, and provide your beds, food, and cooking utensils. It will take a while!

They finally took to the road in an enormous, swaying coach.

Each night after Sally Jay swept out a room, they cooked their own food and slept in their own bed.

For labor, two good mules are worth at least three horses.

But they're not so handsome!

We've been unharmed by highwaymen but robbed by innkeepers!

In Madrid, Jay soon learned from the Spanish Foreign Minister that his stay would probably be futile.

I can't receive you as a minister— your country is not yet a nation! But we may talk informally, Mr. Jay.

For two years John Jay worked hard to promote United States interests. Like John Adams in England, he could unburden himself only to his wife.

He breaks our appointments— won't agree to anything—we are treated like poor relations!

At last Jay left Spain for Paris to play a part in making the peace treaty, then home to become foreign minister in the new American government. But his troubles with Spain were far from over.

With the passage of the Northwest Ordinance, settlers poured into the west as never before. In less than a year, a group of New Englanders bought 1.5 million acres of land...

... from Congress, and sailed down the Ohio River in a fleet headed by the old *Mayflower!*

Once again the *Mayflower* brings settlers to a new land, Ohio!

We will call our settlement Marietta.

Floating downstream was the easiest method of transportation. West of the mountains, all streams led eventually to the great Mississippi River and down to the Spanish port of New Orleans. As the settlers raised crops and had a surplus to sell, it became the outlet for their produce.

Daniel Boone preferred hunting, but other Kentuckians became farmers.

Guess I'll cart my tobacco over the Ohio and arrange to have it boated downriver.

But one day, the boatman came back with bad news.

The Spaniards have closed their port at New Orleans. They're chargin' a tax to take tobacco through — more than it's worth!

They can't do that!

The peace treaty said New Orleans is to be a free port!

That's right! What's our government going to do about it?

What did you do with your cargo?

It's still sittin' there. No way to get it back upstream.

What are we gonna do with our crops? Can't carry them over the mountains.

Once again John Jay, now foreign minister, was faced with the Spanish problem. He talked with the Spanish ambassador.

My country will not even consider opening the mouth of the Mississippi to American traffic!

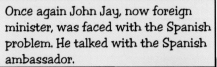

For a year, Jay argued and bargained. He received only one concession.

We might agree that ports in Spain will be free to American ships—if America will agree not to ask us to open the Mississippi.

Jay talked with his advisers.

That is a good bargain! Our eastern merchants are anxious for free ports.

But the westerners will be very angry at such an agreement!

Jay proposed the agreement to Congress, and the westerners were furious. They passed resolutions and held mass meetings. George Rogers Clark spoke.

I'll raise an army and we'll march down and take New Orleans by force!

If the East won't help us, we'll set up our own country!

Benjamin Franklin agreed with the westerners.

A man might as well ask me to sell my street door!

Very well. I will withdraw my proposal.

George Washington and James Madison were alarmed for the future of the Union.

What faith can westerners have in a government that bargains away their most vital interest?

The western states stand on a pivot; the touch of a feather will turn them away.

Our present government commands respect neither from foreign powers nor from its own states!

It is essential that the Articles of Confederation be revised.

At the suggestion of Alexander Hamilton, Congress sent out a call for all states to send delegates to Philadelphia in May 1787, "for the sole and express purpose of revising the Articles of Confederation." All of the states sent delegates except Rhode Island.

It was hot and humid in Philadelphia that May. George Washington, arriving from Virginia, received a special welcome.

Hurrah for General Washington!

His first stop was to call on Benjamin Franklin, 81 years old and recently returned from France.

Come in, come in! I've a new cask of porter* just for your welcome!

Dr. Franklin suffered badly from gout and traveled in a sedan-chair. It was one of the city's sights.

Look! Dr. Franklin!

*A kind of ale.

Every day the porters carried him up the stairs and into the east room of the statehouse.

I brought my chair from Paris. Only form of transportation that doesn't jostle me!

James Madison rode in from New York, where Congress was meeting.

George Washington was unanimously elected president of the convention. Madison, who came to be known as the "father of the constitution," never missed a day's attendance and kept a complete record.

I regret my lack of qualifications for such a task. I hope you will forgive my errors, as they will be unintentional.

The sessions were secret, and so were Madison's notes until Congress authorized their publication in 1840.

Persistent news reporters bothered the delegates.

Is it true, sir, that you are not only revising the Confederation articles ...

... but that you are actually writing a new constitution?

Sorry, I have no comment!

Philadelphia residents were pleased to have the Convention there, and they were interested in the proceedings.

I hear all the states are there but Rhode Island.

Guess they're too busy rioting in Rhode Island to bother.

There's riots in Massachusetts, too.

The westerners are talking about pulling out and going in with Spain.

I hear there's a group in New York State that's bargaining with Canada about joining up with England again!

There's just too many different interests pulling different ways.

The small states are scared the big states will run things—and the big states aren't about to let the little ones tell them what to do!

There's some fine, smart men in the meeting. They'll figure something out.

Old Ben Franklin will pull them together.

Well, it'll take a miracle!

At the convention, Edmund Randolph, governor of Virginia, spoke.

Look at the public countenance, from New Hampshire to Georgia! Are we not on the eve of war, which is only prevented by the hopes from this convention?

Randolph spoke for four hours, presenting the Virginia or Large State Plan for a national government. It proposed an executive branch headed by a president; a legislative branch made up of a two-house congress; and a high court branch. The number of lawmakers allowed for each state would be chosen on the basis of the state's population, which would give the large states control.

The Virginia Plan was debated for days. William Paterson of New Jersey summed up a main objection.

Shall I submit the welfare of New Jersey with five votes in a government where Virginia has 16? Neither my state nor myself will ever submit.

Shall New Jersey have the same right in the nation with Pennsylvania? I say no! It is unjust!

The small states wanted a legislature in which each state, regardless of population, would have the same number of votes.

Roger Sherman, a signer of the Declaration of Independence, was a well-known figure.

Look, there goes Roger Sherman! John Adams called him "that old Puritan—honest as an angel."

And Thomas Jefferson said, "Mr. Sherman of Connecticut, who never said a foolish thing in his life!"

Yes, indeed. It was Roger Sherman who suggested the Great Compromise.

I propose that in the House the proportion of votes should be according to the number of free inhabitants; and in the Senate, each state should have one vote and no more.

But this brought up serious problems. How were slaves to be counted? And what about slavery, anyway? Governor Morris spoke, and Rutledge replied.

I declare slavery to be a nefarious* institution, the curse of heaven.

It is a question of whether the southern states shall or shall not be parties to the Union!

Most northern states had abolished or would soon abolish slavery. Most delegates believed slavery to be morally wrong.

In Massachusetts in 1781, a test case had come before the court involving Quock Walker, a Black slave.

Whereas the Constitution of the Commonwealth of Massachusetts declares all men to be born free and equal, therefore slavery cannot exist here. Quock Walker is a free man.

Thank God!

The delegates' job was to create a constitution that the people would accept. Therefore, another compromise was worked out. It was agreed that five slaves should count the same as three free persons in deciding the number of representatives a state would have. In return, the southern states agreed that importing slaves would not be allowed after 1808.

* extremely wicked, wrong, unjust

34

There were many things to argue about. The hot summer dragged on. Delegates wondered if an agreement would ever be reached. On Independence Day, July 4, there were great celebrations. All over the country there were toasts and congratulations.

The Federal Convention—may the results of their meeting be as glorious as its members are illustrious!

The Grand Convention—may they form a constitution for an eternal Republic!

I'll drink to that!

But in Philadelphia was one of Washington's French officers. He had watched the General leaving the state house.

The look on his face reminded me of his expression during the terrible months at Valley Forge.

At last, unbelievably, a final copy was drawn up on September 17. It was presented to the delegates to be signed.

It will astonish our enemies, who are waiting to hear that our councils are confounded and that our states are on the point of separation.

Often during our sessions I have looked at that sun without being able to tell whether it was rising or setting.

Now I have the happiness to know that it is a rising sun!

Newspapers all over the country published the proposed constitution. Everywhere people discussed it.

What happens now, my dear?

Conventions must be called in each state to vote for or against acceptance. If nine states approve it, it will then become the supreme law.

General Knox (he and his wife were known as "the largest couple in New York") would work hard for its acceptance there.

People will ridicule it—as they did the ark while Noah was building it—but we must convince them it will save them!

If you could get those cannons to Boston, you can do this.

One of the greatest objections to the Constitution was the lack of specific guarantees of certain rights to the people. When it was promised that these would be added, 11 states voted their approval.

In New York, where Alexander Hamilton had led the fight for approval, the people went wild with joy. A great procession was organized.

The state electors voted for a president.

Every elector wrote Washington's name first on his ballot!

How can the government fail, with him in charge?

In New York City, on April 30, 1789, George Washington took the oath as first president of the United States of America.

He wore a plain suit of brown, homespun, American-made wool.

It was a new nation, a new constitution, a new government. At first no one was quite sure what to do. A lot of people decided to call on the new president.

I want a job!

I want to give him my regards.

We're planning to stay for dinner!

Washington consulted James Madison.

They're here at every hour of the day and for every meal. What shall I do?

You'll have to set up rules. Say an open house Tuesdays and Fridays, otherwise only by invitation!

John Adams had been elected vice president. He presided over the Senate.

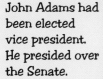

We must take up the important question of a title for addressing the president. It must emphasize dignity and splendor!

I propose "his elective majesty."

I suggest "His Highness the President of the United States and Protector of the Rights of the Same."

For three weeks the Senate debated. Then the House of Representatives refused to go along with the idea of a kingly title, and Washington and others since have been plain "Mr. President."

The House was getting things done. They passed the promised Bill of Rights. People discussed them.

What does it say there about the new Bill of Rights?

They guarantee religious freedom, free speech, a free press, the right of assembly ...

That means we can get together in a meeting and protest what we don't like!

They can't put soldiers in our homes, or search our property, or seize our goods without a warrant, like the Redcoats did.

An accused man can have a fair trial and a jury if he wants it.

And no cruel and unusual punishment!

And we can still have our state militia.

And any powers not specifically given to the federal government belong to the states or to the people.

It's good to have those things spelled out in the Constitution.

Washington appointed Alexander Hamilton to be secretary of the treasury.

This is the most urgent job. We must raise money to run the government and to pay our debts.

I will draw up a plan, sir. I hope it will work.

Hamilton discussed it with Madison.

We must pay the national debts and also the state debts. Otherwise the United States' credit will be ruined.

The southern states that have paid their own debts will be opposed. But they might be won over.

If we vote to establish the permanent capital city in the South, they might vote for the debt plan.

So it was decided. And the new capital city, Washington, D.C., would be located on the banks of the Potomac River in Maryland.

An import tax was voted to be placed on foreign goods coming into the country. But more money would be needed.

What further taxes will be the least unpopular?

I suggest an excise tax on having distilleries and a land tax.

A whiskey tax was imposed in 1791. To some, it was like taxing money. In western Pennsylvania, whiskey was used as money. Perhaps Madison and Hamilton had never been there.

An eastern visitor talked to a Pennsylvania farmer.

Why do you raise all this rye? Is there a market for it?

Well, yes and no. Rye grows well here.

If we packed it over the mountains on horses, it wouldn't sell for enough to pay us. A horse can carry only four bushels of grain.

But a horse can carry 24 bushels after it's made into whiskey. It won't spoil, either!

They used it for money, too—trading "wet goods" for dry goods.

A new axe-head, four yards of cloth, an iron spider*— that'll be two gallons.

Sounds like the price is down a little.

* A type of iron frying pan

These farmers did not see more than a few dollars a year in cash. Whiskey was used for everything.

Money's scarce, Reverend. We brought this year's salary in wet goods.

Thank you, boys, that's fine!

When the farmers protested the tax, Hamilton's answer made them more angry.

I see where Mr. Hamilton says if we don't like paying the tax on whiskey, we can stop drinking so much.

Those Easterners don't know or care what happens out here! We ought to revolt!

We don't just drink it, we live on it!

The farmers wrote petitions and held protest meetings. Finally mobs of disguised men attacked a few tax collectors. This was known as the Whiskey Rebellion.

Maybe the tar and feathers'll teach him a lesson.

Get out of town and don't come back, if you know what's good for you!

Hamilton appealed to President Washington.

This is insurrection! It is spreading to other states! We must show once and for all that the nation rules!

I will call out the militia from New Jersey, Maryland, and Virginia.

Hamilton and Washington rode out to meet with a combined army of 12,000 men.

All this for some Pennsylvania farmers?

Looks like they're using a sledgehammer to kill a fly!

Washington rode back after reviewing the troops. Hamilton led the army through Pennsylvania, but he never found any armed rebels. The leaders had fled. Only two of the people he arrested were found guilty of treason, and Washington later pardoned them.

The most threatening things he found were placed on liberty poles.

Thomas Jefferson had become secretary of state in the new government. He commented.

An insurrection was announced and proclaimed and armed against, but could never be found.

Hamilton and I in the same cabinet are like two cocks in a pit.* We disagree about almost everything.

Yet you both have the good of the country at heart!

But he wants to achieve it through a strong central government and a strong business community. I want strong states and a strong people!

They call those who agree with Hamilton Federalists. Would you call yourself an anti-Federalist?

I prefer Republican or—better, Democratic-Republican.

John Adams was somewhat in-between—a Federalist, but more moderate than Hamilton. Upon Washington's retirement, Adams was elected president in 1796 in a close election. Jefferson became vice president.

I, John Adams, do solemnly swear ...

*cock fighting was a popular entertainment

France and England were at war. France had been a friend of the United States, but now things were different. President Adams conferred with Vice President Jefferson.

The French government has insulted our ambassador! They have seized 80 American ships and their crews!

The people are very angry and demanding war.

Adams sent a message to Congress warning them to prepare for war.

We must arm American merchant vessels! Build up our harbor defenses! We need a strong Navy!

Three American frigates, the *Constellation*, the *Delaware*, and the *Constitution*, were completed in 1798.

A year later the *Constellation*, under the command of Commodore Thomas Truxtun, encountered a French frigate, *L'Insurgente*, in stormy seas.

The *Constellation* immediately attacked.

After half an hour the French ship lowered its flag.

She's striking her colors! We've made a capture!

During two-and-a-half years of undeclared naval warfare, 84 French privateers were captured by American privateers.

The extreme Federalists wanted war. They wanted to keep foreigners out of the country. And they wanted everyone to agree with them. A reporter interviewed one such congressman.

It is patriotism to write in favor of our government—it is sedition to write against it—is that what you say?

And then there are all these foreigners! They come to this country and don't understand our ways and they vote for Jefferson's party! But don't print that!

Yes, sir—no, sir!

Absolutely! Disagreement is treason!

As wartime measures, they rushed through Congress several acts known as the Alien and Sedition Acts. The former gave the President almost unlimited powers to arrest or deport aliens. They increased to 14 years the time necessary to live in the United States before becoming a citizen. The Sedition Act punished with heavy fines or imprisonment any person publishing anything "fake" or "malicious" about the government.

Fifteen editors and printers were arrested. Among them was a Congressman Matthew Lyon of Vermont.

Is it true that you published a letter from a reader calling the president a bully and the Senate stupid?

Certainly, it's true!

Freedom of the press is guaranteed by the Constitution!

But the judge sentenced Congressman Lyon anyway.

One thousand dollars fine or four months in jail!

Lyon went to jail. His friends stormed it. They intended to release him.

We've come to get you out, Matthew!

Thanks, but that's not the way. Use your votes and see that I am reelected to Congress.

Lyon was reelected by a landslide, but he was still in jail.

We'll take up a collection to pay his fine.

I'm afraid it will take a long time for us poor farmers to raise $1,000.

But not all Lyon's friends were in Vermont. One day Senator Stevens Mason of Virginia rode into town.

There's $1,000 in gold in those saddlebags. Many friends of Matthew contributed, including Thomas Jefferson.

His fine paid, Lyon was released.

We must throw the Federalists out of power—and elect Thomas Jefferson president!

Opposition to the Alien and Sedition Acts brought the Democratic-Republican Party together as never before.

President Adams never used the extreme powers given him by the Alien Acts. The Sedition Act expired at the end of his term of office. Resisting great pressure from Hamilton and the extreme Federalists, he kept the country out of a declared war with France. Toward the end of his administration, the government moved to the new federal city.

It was during Washington's presidency that work was begun on the new capital.

Major L'Enfant, you served me well during the war! We would like to employ you to design our federal district and capital.

I would be pleased, my General!

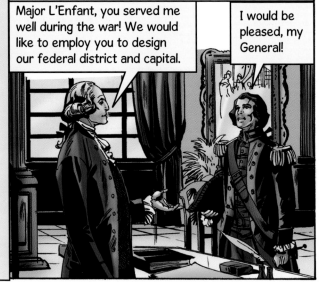

Looking over the land on the Potomac River, L'Enfant was particularly impressed by Jenkins Hill, one day to become Capitol Hill.

It is like a pedestal awaiting its monument!

But L'Enfant's plans were too grand and too expensive for the infant nation to afford.

Please inform Major L'Enfant that his services must be dispensed with.

The site was surveyed by Andrew Ellicott and a Black mathematician and astronomer, Benjamin Banneker.

Building progressed slowly. There were not real streets, and except for the incomplete government buildings, there were only wooden shacks.

Dust in dry weather, a swamp in wet weather, mosquitoes all the time!

But you should see the plans for the president's house!

During Adams' term of office, the White House became habitable. Abigail Adams, arriving from Massachusetts, became lost in the woods.

I can't believe it. Where is the town? This can't be Pennsylvania Avenue!

No, ma'am. I can't find even a path.

They asked help from a slave gathering firewood.

Come this way. I'll show you. It's a mite hard to find.

Pennsylvania Avenue was mostly bushes, mud holes, and tree stumps. The "president's palace" had no lawn, no garden, no fence, and was still unfinished.

Oh, dear!

Keeping house in a new and unfinished residence was not easy.

My dear, it will take 30 servants to keep the place up properly!

The plaster is not dry. We should keep fires in all 13 fireplaces. But wood is very dear hereabouts!

Perhaps I cannot afford to be president on the president's salary.

Perhaps he would not be president very much longer. There was a presidential election coming up.

What are the issues?

The Democratic-Republicans accused the Federalists of running the country for the rich aristocrats—and the Federalists say the Republicans will turn it over to a mob of revolutionaries!

You can take your pick—John Adams or Thomas Jefferson.

Is it true we don't vote directly for the candidates?

That's right—we vote for electors. You pick the electors who want the same candidate you want.

People all over the country went to the polls and picked electors. In each state the electors met and voted. Then from every state, express-riders sped away to Washington.

It was the duty of Thomas Jefferson, vice-president and chairman of the Senate, to announce the results.

Jefferson 73, Burr 73, Adams 65

A tie!

It's a tie!

The Republicans had intended to elect Jefferson president, Aaron Burr vice president. But it was a tie. And in case of a tie, the Constitution said the House of Representatives must decide.

The House of Representatives met and voted.

The vote is a tie!

Something was wrong with the heat. The hall was cold. They shivered and voted again.

The vote is a tie!

They sent out for food. They stayed all night. Still a tie vote. They went home and came back again. After 35 ballots, the results were the same.

After six days, on the 36th ballot, James Bayard of Delaware rose.

I am switching Delaware's vote to Thomas Jefferson of Virginia!

At last the country had a new president.

"The election of Mr. Jefferson has produced the liveliest feelings of joy," reported the *New York Gazette*. All over the country his supporters celebrated.

Rejoice, Columbia's sons, rejoice,
To tyrants never bend the knee;
But join with heart, and soul and voice,
For Jefferson and liberty.

Before the revolution, and through the long years, John Adams had worked for the country. He had put its interests above party politics, and his own party had turned against him. He was ready to retire.

At dawn on Inauguration Day, his carriage rolled away from Washington, taking him home to Massachusetts and his beloved family.